TREEMENDOUS

Diary of a Not Yet Mighty Oak

BRIDGET HEOS

ILLUSTRATED BY MIKE CICCOTELLO

Crown Books for Young Readers
New York

For Jack Brewster,
who is also treemendous!
—B.H.

For Mom,
thanks for giving me
everything I needed to grow.
—M.C.

Text copyright © 2021 by Bridget Heos
Jacket art and interior illustrations copyright © 2021 by Mike Ciccotello

All rights reserved. Published in the United States by Crown Books for Young Readers, an imprint of
Random House Children's Books, a division of Penguin Random House LLC, New York.

Crown and the colophon are registered trademarks of Penguin Random House LLC.

Visit us on the Web! rhcbooks.com

Educators and librarians, for a variety of teaching tools, visit us at RHTeachersLibrarians.com

Library of Congress Cataloging-in-Publication Data
Names: Heos, Bridget, author. | Ciccotello, Mike, illustrator.
Title: Treemendous : diary of a not yet mighty oak / Bridget Heos ; illustrated by Mike Ciccotello.
Description: First edition. | New York : Crown Books for Young Readers,
[2021] | Includes bibliographical references. | Audience: Ages 3–7. | Audience: Grades K–1. |
Summary: Illustrates the life of a tiny acorn growing up to be a tall oak tree.
Identifiers: LCCN 2020010535 (print) | LCCN 2020010536 (ebook) | ISBN 978-0-525-57936-6 (hardcover) |
ISBN 978-0-525-57937-3 (library binding) | ISBN 978-0-525-57938-0 (ebook)
Subjects: CYAC: Oak—Fiction. | Trees—Fiction. | Growth—Fiction.
Classification: LCC PZ7.H4118 Tr 2021 (print) | LCC PZ7.H4118 (ebook) | DDC [E]—dc23

The text of this book is set in 16-point New Century Schoolbook.
The illustrations in this book were created digitally using the application Procreate on an iPad Pro with an Apple Pencil.

MANUFACTURED IN CHINA
10 9 8 7 6 5 4 3 2 1
First Edition

YEAR 1, DAY 1 • APRIL 5

Hello, world!

They say that from the smallest acorn,
the mightiest oak tree grows. I hope that's true.

YEAR 2 • APRIL 5

I'm turning one today! Oh, how I wish to be a tree like all my
relatives in the forest. That's my grandmother over there.
And those are my aunts and uncles.

   Of course, there are other families in the forest, too, like:
   the Walnuts (they're a little nutty, if you ask me),
   the Florals (which have a certain buzz about them),
   and the Pines (that one family who always goes
overboard with Christmas decorations).

Though the forest is filled with trees,
I mainly hang out with my brothers and
sisters. We're just an average family—all
10,000 of us.

My twigmates and I are especially close . . .
sometimes too close. Ugh, scootch over!

SEPTEMBER 22

It's getting cooler. One by one—
plink!—my brothers and sisters fall,
until finally . . .

Whee!

It's myyyyyy tuuuuuurn!

Um, now what?

SEPTEMBER 24

By Mom's side, we have it made in the shade!
But each of us must find our own place in the sun.

OCTOBER 10

I catch a ride with a furry friend.

NOVEMBER 1

Oh, no! I've lost my cap. And where is that squirrel, anyway? It hid me and then never came back. Worst game of hide-and-seek ever!

Sigh. Might as well snuggle in and catch some ZZZZZZZZZZZZZZZs.

leaves

stem

root

YEAR 3 • MARCH 23

I'm rested and ready for spring.
In fact, I'm bursting with energy!
Whoa!

I did it! I sprouted!
Root? Check.
Stem? Check.
Leaves? Check. Check. Check.

Hey, I'm growing right next to
Grandma. And one of the Pine seedlings.
The three of us spend our days soaking
up the sun! Ah, that's the stuff!

OCTOBER 14

I just noticed I'm growing
all these little buds.

What's up, Bud? Hello
there, Bud. Oh, hey, Bud!

I wonder what that's
all about.

It's getting c-c-cold! Pine Tree's leaves are
still green as can be. But mine are changing color.
Ooh la la, I'm a redhead now!
Yawn. Getting sleepy.

Ding ding ding! It's spring spring spring!

My buds are bursting into stems and leaves. Now I'm taller . . . and more gorgeous!

What makes my leaves so shiny and green? Amazing chlorophyll allows my leaves to absorb sunlight and carbon dioxide from the air. Then poof! Like magic, the sunlight changes the water and carbon dioxide into sugar, aka tree food. Sweet!

This is called photosynthesis. It's complicated. *I'm* complicated.

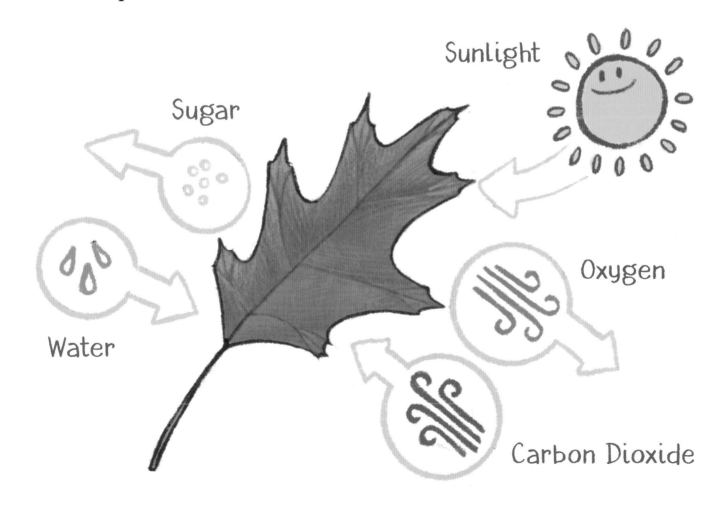

Sunlight

Sugar

Water

Oxygen

Carbon Dioxide

SEPTEMBER 3

Good morning!

And what a morning it is.

The sun is shining.

The birds are singing.

Insects are attacking me.

Hey, buzz off! Luckily, I'm what you call thick-skinned.
Each year I grow new layers of wood and bark. My new
bark carries food to all my parts. My old bark protects me
from pests. Shoo! Shoo!

Sigh . . . I just have so many layers!

YEAR 5 • APRIL 9

I'm four and a half feet
tall now, and a little thicker.
Last year's new bark is now
old bark, and last year's sapwood
is now heartwood, which helps
me stand straight and tall like
the fine young tree I am.

My new layer of sapwood
carries water up and
down my trunk.
The rainwater flows
up through my roots,
trunks, branches, and
twigs as if my leaves
are drinking it through
a straw. Gulp!

Ahhh. Refreshing!

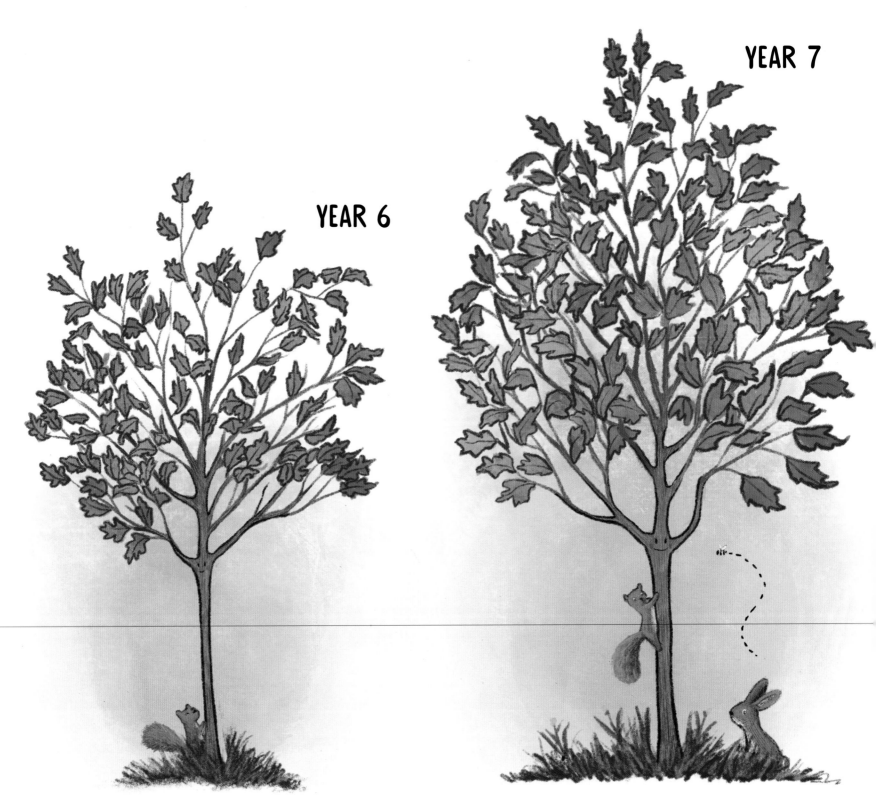

YEAR 6

YEAR 7

Each spring and summer, I grow   and grow

YEAR 9

and grow until . . .

YEAR 10 • APRIL 5

I'm a ten-year-old tree standing twenty feet tall! You know what they say, time flies when you're having sun.

The great thing is, I've grown so tall that now I can see Mom! And my brothers and sisters. And the Pines! And Walnuts! And Florals!

APRIL 26

I feel like I'm part of something big now.

Remember how I said my leaves absorb carbon dioxide?

Well, too much carbon dioxide in the air causes global warming.

Trees slow down global warming!

At the same time, my leaves release oxygen, which animals need to breathe. Not to be sappy, but trees make the world a better place.

JUNE 28

It's hard to believe that I started
out as a teeny tiny acorn, and
now I'm a mighty oak.

Well, almost.

YEAR 20 • APRIL 5

I've started sprouting flowers!
Just like the Florals.

   Oh, my heartwood! Some of
my flowers are turning into little
acorns! They look just like I did
as a seed.

I can't wait to
be a mighty oak,
just like Mom!

ANATOMY OF ME (AN OAK TREE)

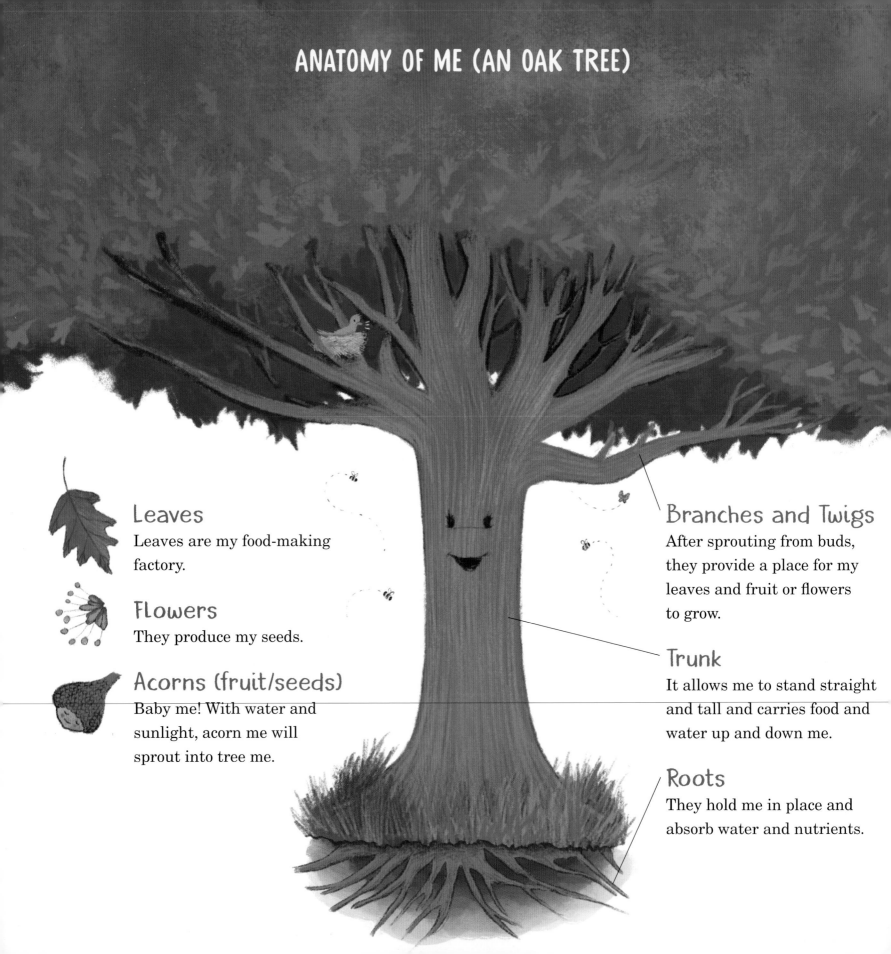

Leaves
Leaves are my food-making factory.

Flowers
They produce my seeds.

Acorns (fruit/seeds)
Baby me! With water and sunlight, acorn me will sprout into tree me.

Branches and Twigs
After sprouting from buds, they provide a place for my leaves and fruit or flowers to grow.

Trunk
It allows me to stand straight and tall and carries food and water up and down me.

Roots
They hold me in place and absorb water and nutrients.

GETTING TO THE HEART(WOOD) OF ME

Heartwood
Once sapwood, it is now deadwood. As long as I am healthy, it does not decay, but rather remains at the center of me, helping me stand straight.

Sapwood
My new layer of wood carries water up my trunk to my leaves.

Cambium cell layer
My wood and bark factory! It produces new layers in both directions: the inner bark moving outward and the sapwood moving inward.

Inner bark
My new layer of bark carries food made in my leaves throughout the tree.

Outer bark
Once inner bark, it now forms the thick layer that protects me from insects, heat, and cold.

MY LiFE

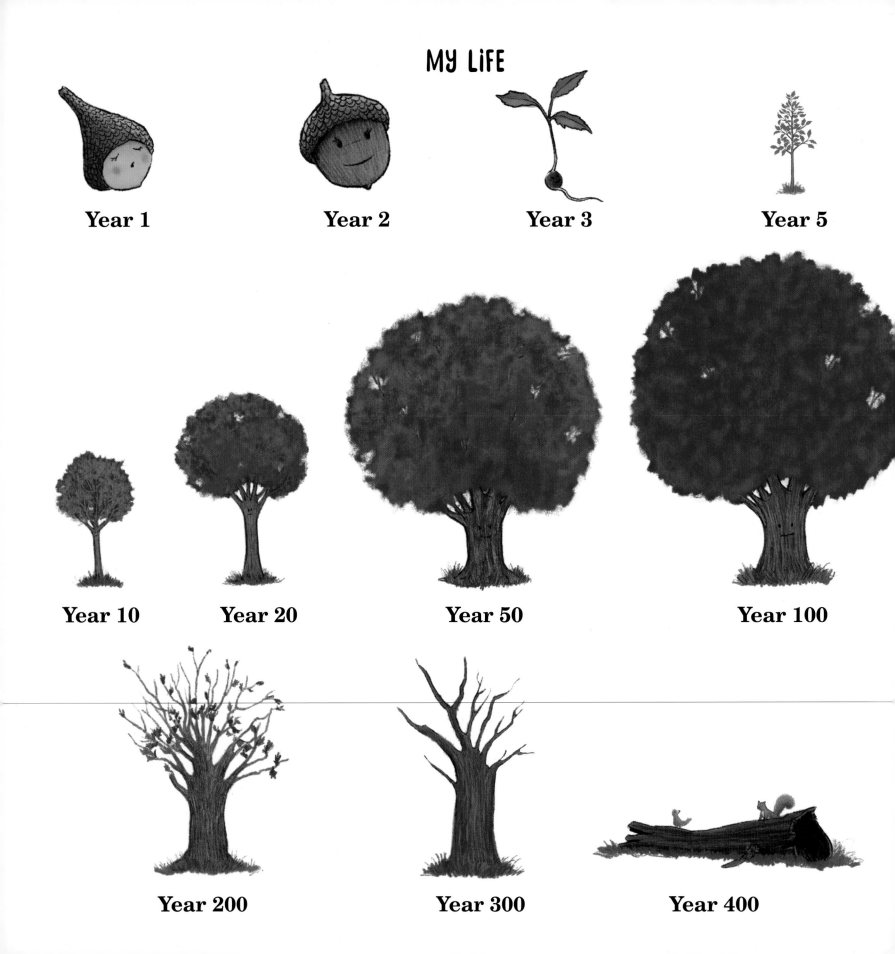

Year 1

Year 2

Year 3

Year 5

Year 10

Year 20

Year 50

Year 100

Year 200

Year 300

Year 400

FOR FURTHER EXPLORATION

BOOKS

Bang, Molly, and Penny Chisholm. *Living Sunlight: How Plants Bring the Earth to Life.* New York: The Blue Sky Press, 2009.

Bulla, Clyde Robert. *A Tree Is a Plant.* New York: Harper, 2016 (revised edition).

Karas, G. Brian. *As an Oak Tree Grows.* New York: Nancy Paulsen Books, 2014.

Napoli, Donna Jo. *Mama Miti: Wangari Maathai and the Trees of Kenya.* New York: Simon & Schuster, 2010.

Schaefer, Lola M., and Adam Schaefer. *Because of an Acorn.* San Francisco: Chronicle, 2016.

Socha, Piotr, and Wojciech Grajkowski. *Trees: A Rooted History.* New York: Abrams, 2019.

WEBSITES

arborday.org/kids
Learn more about trees.

climatekids.nasa.gov
Learn about climate change and things you can do to help, such as planting a tree!

discovertheforest.org
Find a forest to explore nearby.